Columbia University

Contributions to Education

Teachers College Series

No. 438

AMS PRESS
NEW YORK

INFLUENCE OF REGULARLY INTERPOLATED TIME INTERVALS UPON SUBSEQUENT LEARNING

By
IRVING LORGE

TEACHERS COLLEGE, COLUMBIA UNIVERSITY
CONTRIBUTIONS TO EDUCATION, NO. 438

183811

BUREAU OF PUBLICATIONS
Teachers College, Columbia University
NEW YORK CITY
1930

Library of Congress Cataloging in Publication Data

Lorge, Irving, 1905–
    Influence of regularly interpolated time intervals
upon subsequent learning.

    Reprint of the 1930 ed., issued in series: Teachers
College, Columbia University. Contributions to
education, no. 438.
    Originally presented as the author's thesis, Columbia.
    Bibliography: p.
    1. Educational psychology. 2. Study, Method of.
I. Title. II. Series: Columbia University. Teachers
College. Contributions to education, no. 438.
LB1026.L6   1972   370.15'2   73-177011
ISBN 0-404-55438-5

Reprinted by Special Arrangement with Teachers
College Press, New York, New York

From the edition of 1930, New York
First AMS edition published in 1972
Manufactured in the United States

AMS PRESS, INC.
NEW YORK, N. Y.   10003

ACKNOWLEDGMENTS

Formulas of thanks are inadequate expressions to Dr. Arthur I. Gates and Dr. Henry E. Garrett for their aid, to Dr. Henry A. Ruger for his unstinted advice, and to Dr. E. L. Thorndike for his suggestion of the problem and his advice during the course of the study.

To Dr. Ella Woodyard for her aid in experimentation and to the many subjects who perforce remain anonymous, I express my appreciation.

I. L.

Teachers College
Columbia University
April, 1930

CONTENTS

SECTION I

INTRODUCTION

Distribution of practice generally makes for economy. Under distribution of practice a fact is learned, or a skill acquired, with less effort than if the practice were massed.

Massed practice is that condition of learning in which each trial is immediately succeeded by another trial without the intervention of any period of time between the successive trials. In contradistinction to massed practice is the condition of distributed practice. Under distribution of practice an interval is interpolated between successive trials.

Although there is but one type of massed or continuous practice, there are infinite variations of distributed practice. There may be variations in the duration of the interval. There may be variations in the frequency of interpolation of an interval. And there may be variation in the stage of the practice at which interpolations are introduced or withdrawn.

Ruch ['28] * in his summary of the experimental literature on distribution and massing of practice for humans finds that "the following factors have received experimental consideration and are of major importance: first, the general characteristics of the distribution of practice (number and length of periods, intervals between periods, degree of learning being considered, etc.); second, the type of material being learned; third, the age of the subjects; fourth, criterion or aim of the learning (immediate or delayed recall, speed, accuracy, and amount of recall, improvement, etc.); fifth, the order of repetitions within a practice period (whole *vs.* part order); sixth, the manner of studying; seventh, the stage of learning (whether the distribution is equally effective at the initial and final stages of learning and in the exercise of a well learned habit)."

The first and seventh factors are the subject of this investigation. Distributed practice will be used to discover whether the distribution is effective at the initial and final stages of learning.

* For summaries of the relevant literature see especially Warden ['22] and Ruch ['28].

1

Any study in distribution must consider at least the following five variables:

   a. The duration of the interpolated interval.

   b. The frequency of interpolations.

   c. The unit of practice.

   d. The number of units of practice.

   e. The stage of learning at which interpolations are introduced.

The specific type of distributed practice considered in this investigation is that form of distribution in which a constant time interval is regularly interpolated after each constant unit of practice. It is an established fact that groups learning under this particular type of distribution learn a fact or acquire a skill in fewer units of practice than do groups learning the same fact, or practicing the same skill, under massed or continuous practice. The literature, however, is not conclusive as to whether distributed practice results in efficiency only at the beginning of learning, or whether such efficiency is noted at later stages of practice, or whether there is an additional increment to efficiency due to each successive interpolation of interval.

The specific problem of this study is to ascertain what differences in efficiency, if any, result at trials subsequent to each regular interpolation of a constant time interval in a practice series.

The experiment will always be concerned with the achievement after the same number of units of practice of two equal groups— a group that practiced under distribution, and a group that practiced under massed or continuous practice. Let the symbol representing the achievement at trial r of the group learning under massing be A_{M_r}. This symbol A_{M_r} is then read as the achievement of the group learning under massing at trial r. In a corresponding manner, the symbol A_{D_r} is read as the achievement of the group learning under the distributed practice specific to this study at trial r. The difference between A_{M_r} and A_{D_r} would indicate that superiority or inferiority of the M or the D condition which differentiates the two achievements. Since difference is usually in favor of the D group a symbol S_{D_r} will represent the observed superiority at trial r of A_{D_r} over A_{M_r}. The relationship that exists is $S_{D_r} = A_{D_r} - A_{M_r}$.

Since each A_{D_r} is attained after a unit interval, D, has been interpolated, A_{D_1} is the achievement after the first interpolation;

A_{D_1} the achievement after the second interpolation; and so on to A_{D_n}. Then S_{D_2}, which equals $A_{D_2} - A_{M_2}$, is the observed superiority of a group which had as its only differentiating factor the interpolated interval. Similarly S_{D_3}, which represents the difference between A_{D_3} and A_{M_3}, is the observed superiority due to the first interval and the second interval. Each S_{D_r} then indicates an observed superiority at trial r of the D group over the M group.

Is this superiority at trial r due to the cumulative effect of the interpolation of interval after trial 1, 2, 3, and so on to the interpolation after trial $(r-1)$?

Is there some trial after which S_{D_r} does not increase over $S_{D_{(r-1)}}$?

SECTION II

SNODDY'S RESULTS AND CONCLUSIONS

Snoddy ['26] allowed groups to trace a maze under conditions of distributed and of massed practice. The maze was the stabilimeter, an adaptation made by Snoddy of the conventional mirror-drawing experiment. Three groups were used: the first, the M group, practiced the maze under massing—twenty trials without any time interval between successive trials; the second, the D group, practiced the maze under distribution— a constant interval of one minute being interpolated regularly between successive trials; the third group, the T group, also practiced under conditions of regular distribution but the regularly interpolated interval in this instance was twenty-four hours.

The number of errors made in a circuit plus the number of seconds taken to complete a circuit constituted the score which Snoddy terms the "raw" score. Since improvement is shown by a smaller raw score, Snoddy uses for his reported results a score that is one thousand times the reciprocal of the "raw" score. This reciprocal score he calls the "conductance" score. The conductance score, by the device of reciprocals, indicates improvement by means of larger scores at later trials.

In Table I there are reproduced the median conductance scores for Snoddy's three groups working under the different conditions of practice.

The median achievement of each group is plotted sequentially against trials. Three curves of achievement are obtained: the curve of A_{M_r}, the curve of A_{D_r}, and the curve of the A_{T_r}, where the symbol

A_{M_r} represents the achievement at trial r of the group practicing the stabilimeter under massed conditions;

A_{D_r} represents the achievement at trial r of the group practicing the stabilimeter under conditions of regular interpolation of a constant time interval of duration D (or one minute) after each constant unit of practice;

A_{T_r} represents the achievement at trial r of the group practicing

4

TABLE I.   Median conductance scores after Snoddy [1926, Table 2, page 7]
indicating achievement at each trial

Trial	M	D	T
	The interval regularly interpolated after each trial		
	Zero	One Minute	One Day
1	5.0	5.0	5.0
2	6.1	8.7	11.4
3	7.7	10.4	14.4
4	8.5	12.7	15.9
5	10.0	14.3	18.0
6	10.5	16.1	20.0
7	11.2	17.1	20.6
8	12.3	17.2	21.8
9	11.9	18.2	22.1
10	13.1	18.9	22.0
11	13.7	20.0	23.1
12	13.7	20.8	23.9
13	14.9	20.8	24.5
14	15.4	22.0	24.8
15	15.2	22.4	25.4
16	15.4	21.4	25.7
17	16.1	23.0	25.5
18	15.9	23.8	27.6
19	16.7	24.2	27.0
20	16.7	22.9	26.7

DIAGRAM I.   Graphic representation of Table I

the stabilimeter under conditions of regular interpolation of a constant time interval of duration T (twenty-four hours) after each constant unit of practice.

Symbol A_{M_r} can be interpreted in a manner analogous to that of the other two symbols, as representing achievement at trial r of a group practicing under conditions of regular interpolation of a constant time interval of duration M (or zero) after each constant unit of practice.

The three curves show improvement against trials (Diagram I). Each group does learn under its own condition of practice, the achievement of the group having interpolations of T and D (respectively twenty-four hour intervals and one minute intervals) being greater at each trial than the achievement of the group practicing under massing (or under conditions of interpolating an interval of duration M, or zero).

The observed superiority of the achievement of the group having a regular interval of twenty-four hours interpolated after each unit of practice is the difference between A_{T_r} and A_{M_r} at each trial. Let the symbol of such superiority be S_{T_r}. Then the relationship between superiority due to T and the achievements is

$$S_{T_r} = A_{T_r} - A_{M_r}.$$

In this manner S_{T_2} represents the superiority observed in the achievement at trial 2 of the group having a twenty-four hour interval after trial 1 over the achievement of a group having no interpolation of interval. The plot of S_{T_1} and S_{T_2} and so on to S_{T_r} would represent the superiority observed after each interpolation. This plot would give the trend of superiority observed after each additional interval T and the subsequent trial. In a similar manner the relationship

$$S_{D_r} = A_{D_r} - A_{M_r}$$

would represent the superiority observed subsequent to each interpolation of an interval of duration D (or one minute) over the achievement of the group practicing under the condition M.

A measure of the superiority observed at each trial for each condition of regular distribution over massing is obtained—one the S_{D_r}, the other the S_{T_r}. Table II gives these observed superiorities, trial for trial.

TABLE II. The observed superiority of achievement under condition of regularly interpolating a constant time interval of duration D and T (one minute and one day respectively) after each trial over the achievement under condition of massing. The achievements were in terms of conductance scores [Snoddy 1926].

Trial	S_{Dr}	S_{Tr}
1	0.0	0.0
2	2.6	5.3
3	2.7	6.7
4	4.2	7.4
5	4.3	8.0
6	5.6	9.5
7	5.9	9.4
8	4.9	9.5
9	4.9	10.2
10	5.8	8.9
11	6.3	9.4
12	7.1	10.2
13	5.9	9.6
14	6.6	9.4
15	7.2	10.2
16	6.0	10.3
17	6.9	9.4
18	7.9	11.7
19	7.5	10.3
20	6.2	10.0

DIAGRAM II. Graphic representation of Table II

The plot of S_{Tr} and of S_{Dr} shows the trend (Diagram II).

The trend of S_{Tr} and the trend of S_{Dr} show that, as measured by the difference in conductance score, the observed superiority is becoming greater and greater after each successive trial.

The magnitude of the increment in superiority after trial 6 or 7, however, is not so great as it was at the trials prior to the sixth or seventh. Is it possible that the intervals interpolated after trials 7, 8, and so on have no further effect? Snoddy believes that superiority from trials 7 through 20 is not attributable to the intervals interpolated after the sixth trial, for he has concluded on the basis of these data that "in case time intervals separate the circuits, the improvement in the earlier part of the practice will be a positive function of the length of the time interval. The rate of improvement is a function of the length of the time interval only during the early part of the practice, when the coordination pattern is being built. Beyond this early adaptation stage the improvement is a function of the number of repetitions. For convenience of description we have called the early stage of the curve, where the improvement depends upon more than repetition alone, the 'adaptation' stage, and the remainder of the curve where improvement is a function of repetition alone, the 'facilitation' stage." ['26, p. 8.]

This conclusion seems unjustifiable from experiments to be described in Sections IV to XI, and also from Snoddy's own results, as will be shown in the next section.

SECTION III

AN ANALYSIS OF SNODDY'S DATA

The conductance score used by Snoddy and the raw score from which it was derived are connected by the relationship

$$\text{Conductance score} = \frac{1000}{\text{Raw score}}.$$

From this relationship, it follows that the

$$\text{Raw score} = \frac{1000}{\text{Conductance score}}.$$

The raw score derived from Snoddy's median conductance score data will be treated in the same manner as the conductance score. As in the preceding section, the meaning of A_{M_r}, A_{D_r}, and A_{T_r} will be the achievement at trial r under condition of regular interpolation, after a constant unit of practice, of a constant time interval (of duration M, D, and T, or of zero, one minute, and one day, respectively).

The raw score, it must be noted, in contradistinction to the conductance score, shows improvement by a smaller score at subsequent trials. The observed superiority of one type of distribution over massing will be indicated by the amount of score saved, i.e., observed superiority will be indicated when the difference $A_{D_r} - A_{M_r}$ is negative.

The observed superiority will be represented by the symbols S_{D_r} and S_{T_r} which represent the relationship $A_{D_r} - A_{M_r}$, and $A_{T_r} - A_{M_r}$ respectively.

The achievements of the M, D, and T groups (Table III) plotted against trials show that whereas each group improves at each successive trial, the groups practicing under conditions of a regular distribution of T and D gain and maintain a control of the maze in excess of that of the M group (Diagram III).

The observed superiority of the T and D groups over the M group (Table IV), shown in the graph of S_{D_r} and S_{T_r}, indicates

TABLE III. Median raw scores derived from Snoddy median conductance scores [1926, Table 2, page 7] indicating achievement at each trial.

Trial	M Zero	D One Minute	T One Day
	The interval regularly interpolated after each trial		
1	200.0	200.0	200.0
2	163.9	114.9	87.7
3	129.9	96.2	69.4
4	117.6	78.7	62.9
5	100.0	70.0	55.6
6	95.2	62.1	50.0
7	89.3	58.5	48.5
8	81.3	58.1	45.9
9	84.0	54.9	45.2
10	76.3	52.9	45.5
11	73.0	50.0	43.3
12	73.0	48.1	41.8
13	67.1	48.1	40.8
14	64.9	45.5	40.3
15	65.8	44.6	39.4
16	64.9	46.7	38.9
17	62.1	43.5	39.2
18	62.9	42.0	36.2
19	59.9	41.3	37.0
20	59.9	43.7	37.5

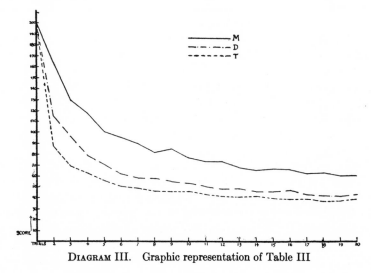

DIAGRAM III. Graphic representation of Table III

that the observed superiority is at maximum at trial 2 (Diagram IV). At trials subsequent to the second the observed superiority is diminished. That is, there is a greater reduction in the time and in the errors (or at least in the composite of them used as a score) in the second trial as an effect of D and T than there is later on.

TABLE IV. The observed superiority of achievement under condition of regularly interpolating a constant time interval of duration D and T (one minute and one day respectively) after each trial over the achievement under condition of massing. The achievements were in terms of raw scores derived from the conductance scores of Snoddy [1926].

Trial	S_{D_r}	S_{T_r}
1	0.0	0.0
2	49.0	76.2
3	33.7	60.5
4	38.9	54.7
5	30.0	44.4
6	33.1	45.2
7	30.8	40.8
8	23.2	35.4
9	29.1	38.8
10	23.4	30.8
11	23.0	29.7
12	24.9	31.2
13	19.0	26.3
14	19.4	24.6
15	21.2	26.4
16	18.2	26.0
17	18.6	22.9
18	20.9	26.7
19	18.6	22.9
20	16.2	22.4

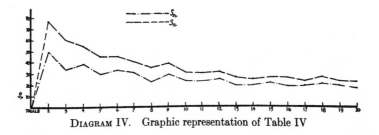

DIAGRAM IV. Graphic representation of Table IV

SECTION IV

NEW EXPERIMENTS IN MIRROR DRAWING

Several groups of subjects practiced tracing the Snoddy maze under distribution in which a constant time interval was regularly interpolated after each constant unit of practice.

The apparatus was the stabilimeter which consisted "of a tracing instrument involving a path to be traced, a mirror producing a good image, a soft stylus to be used pencil-fashion for tracing the path, and an apparatus for counting electric impulses.

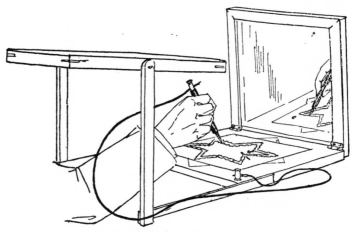

FIGURE 1.   The stabilimeter in use

The tracing instrument involves a sheet of brass, from which has been cut a star-shaped path one-fourth inch in width.   The brass sheet is mounted upon a heavy glass plate.   Niches are cut in the sides of the path to prevent sliding of the stylus along the edge of the path (see Figure 1).   Electric connections are made between the brass plate, the stylus, and the electric counter." [Snoddy, 1926]. *   Throughout this experiment two Stoelting counters

* We wish to thank Dr. Snoddy for his cooperation in building the stabilimeters used in this experiment.

have been used alternately, by means of a double throw, double pole, knife switch.

The maze, instead of being presented without any of the lanes parallel to the subject as in Snoddy's experiment, was rotated through an angle of 90°, so that four of the lanes of the star were parallel with the horizontal axis of the subject. This change in procedure was primarily to change the difficulty of the problem.

Direct vision of the star to be traced was obstructed by a screen, 11⅝ inches by 11⅝ inches, placed 17½ inches from the mirror, and 10½ inches from the table. The screen was arranged so as to

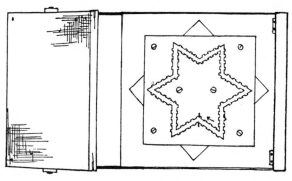

FIGURE 2. Top view of stabilimeter

assure vision of the mirrored image of the maze, but not to permit direct vision of the path. The apparatus was lighted by a desk lamp using a 110-volt frosted bulb.

The brass plate was marked with a black arrow to indicate the direction of the circuit, and by two black lines to indicate the beginning of the circuit (see Figure 2).

The directions which were given before the subject had the stylus in hand were: "Do you see the star in the mirror? You are to trace the star with this stylus in such a way as to avoid touching either brass plate. You are to go in the direction indicated by the black arrow. From time to time you will be told to go either faster or slower. In that event simply follow directions. Is that clear?" The subject was given the stylus, which was placed at the beginning of the maze. Then the subject was asked "Ready?" and then told "Go!" Time was taken to the nearest second by a stop watch.

Snoddy's technique was followed in pacing the subject: The time (in seconds) and the errors (in electrical impulses) were kept approximately equal, by telling the subject to go faster when the number of seconds was in excess of the number of errors; and by telling the subject to go slower when the number of errors was in excess of the number of seconds.

The sum of the errors and the time gives a score which Snoddy calls the raw score. This raw score has been used throughout the experiment in preference to the reciprocals of the raw score which Snoddy uses.*

The reciprocals of the raw scores in our experiment would give curves much like those of Snoddy. See Diagram V-a.

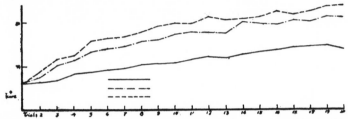

DIAGRAM V-a.   Mean conductance scores (reciprocal of raw scores) derived from the data of Table V

The groups practicing the maze were equated on the basis of score at the first trial.† Thereafter each group practiced the maze under its own condition of distribution. One group practiced without the intervention of any interval of time between successive practices, while the other two groups practiced under condition of interpolation of a constant time interval, after each constant unit of practice, of one minute and twenty-four hours respectively.

* While differences between 6 and 5, 5 and 4, 4 and 3, and 3 and 2 are all equal to 1, differences between the corresponding reciprocals ⅙ and ⅕, ⅕ and ¼, ¼ and ⅓, and ⅓ and ½ are equal to —.034, —.050, —.083, and —.167; so that the higher the scores between which differences of reciprocals are computed, the less the difference between such reciprocals. Since the reciprocal is determined on the scores that are successively becoming less and less, the differences are becoming greater and greater. This accounts for the increase in the superiority of the distribution at trials subsequent to the second when measured by the conductance score. Neither the raw score nor its reciprocal, the conductance score, is entirely suitable for use with our problem. The raw score is an indefinite mixture of speed and errors. Its reciprocal is a still more indefinite mixture of amount produced per unit of time and quality of product. The experiments of Sections V–VII are free from such ambiguity.

† Since the correlations between the CAVD level score (a measure of intelligence) and age and between CAVD level score and initial trial and between age and initial score were low, the groups were equated on the basis of mean initial score. The characteristics of the groups, mean age, mean level score, and the technic of sampling are given in Appendix A.

The mean achievement at trial r of each group is represented by the symbols A_{M_r}, A_{D_r}, and A_{T_r}. These symbols represent the mean achievement at trial r of a group that practiced the maze under conditions of interpolating after each unit of practice a constant time interval of duration M, D, or T (zero,* one minute, and one day respectively).

The achievement at each trial of each group is given in Table V, the plot of the achievements giving the learning curves in Diagram V-b.

The learning curves show that each group improves with practice although the groups having regular interpolations of one minute and of twenty-four hours after each unit of practice achieve lower scores at each trial than does the group practicing under conditions of massing. The lower the score, the better the degree of mastery of the maze.

The observed superiority of the D group over M, as well as the observed superiority of the T group over M, is the amount saved. These superiorities are given by the relationships

$$S_{D_r} = A_{D_r} - A_{M_r}$$
$$S_{T_r} = A_{T_r} - A_{M_r}.$$

The observed superiority of T and D over M are given in Table VI. The trend of the observed superiority is obtained by plotting the S_{D_r} and S_{T_r} respectively against trials. Diagram VI showing this trend indicates that the maximum superiority observed is at trial 3 under each condition of regular distribution.

At trials subsequent to the third the superiority diminishes continuously throughout the length of the series. The superiority observable at trial 2 is augmented at trial 3; thereafter it is diminished.

It has been shown on the basis of the raw score data derived from Snoddy that diminution takes place at trial 3 and all subsequent trials. When the maze is presented in a different manner, the observed superiority is augmented at trial 3, although at subsequent trials diminution is observed.

---

* Since the subjects were told to stop after each unit of practice, and directed to begin the next trial, the time intervening between two successive units of practice was not actually zero. A record was kept of the time required to say "Stop. Go." The mean time required to give these orders was 2 ⅕ seconds. This 2 ⅕ seconds was the best approximation to zero that could be obtained.

TABLE V.　The mean raw score (and the sigma of the mean raw score) derived from the experiment with three groups practicing the rotated stabilimeter under conditions of regularly interpolating after each trial a constant time interval of *M*, *D*, or *T* (zero, one minute, and one day, respectively).

	Mean Achievement			Standard Deviation of the Mean		
	M	*D*	*T*	*M*	*D*	*T*
		The interval regularly interpolated after each trial				
Trial	Zero	One Minute	One Day	Zero	One Minute	One Day
1	162.68	161.37	162.84	15.20	14.00	14.70
2	150.42	131.26	113.89	14.15	13.31	9.44
3	144.05	98.89	87.16	10.73	5.92	5.42
4	120.63	88.79	79.74	8.16	6.84	6.42
5	111.63	76.11	63.16	7.42	4.00	4.25
6	110.05	71.53	61.21	7.01	3.45	3.80
7	105.00	69.00	59.63	5.43	7.84	2.46
8	97.16	63.68	56.21	6.27	4.74	3.59
9	94.84	62.47	52.26	5.11	4.19	3.32
10	93.00	58.00	50.63	6.47	4.47	2.25
11	87.79	56.21	50.65	4.25	3.63	2.64
12	82.74	56.74	47.05	4.31	3.51	2.34
13	83.74	57.63	48.84	4.83	3.46	1.45
14	78.84	49.84	47.95	3.71	3.21	1.75
15	75.95	50.79	47.26	3.60	2.83	2.41
16	72.26	51.47	44.53	3.68	3.67	2.49
17	70.58	48.68	45.79	3.19	3.65	2.12
18	69.16	49.79	44.56	2.94	3.44	2.14
19	67.68	46.89	42.42	3.71	2.67	1.80
20	71.95	47.32	41.89	3.69	3.69	2.02

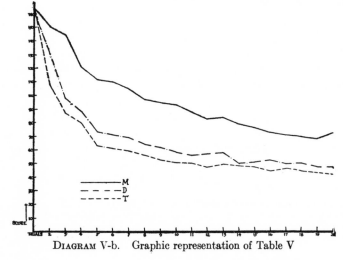

DIAGRAM V-b.　Graphic representation of Table V

No generalization as to which trial will show the greatest superiority for time interpolation seems warranted on the basis of the stabilimeter data.

TABLE VI. The observed superiority of achievement under condition of regularly interpolating a constant time interval of duration D and T (one minute and one day respectively) after each trial over the achievement under condition of massing. The achievements were the raw scores derived from the experiment on the rotated stabilimeter.

Trial	S_{D_r}	S_{T_r}
1	1.32	—.16
2	19.06	36.33
3	45.16	56.89
4	31.84	40.89
5	35.33	48.47
6	38.53	48.84
7	36.00	45.37
8	33.47	40.95
9	32.37	42.58
10	35.00	42.37
11	31.58	37.14
12	26.00	35.68
13	26.14	34.92
14	29.00	30.89
15	25.16	28.68
16	20.79	27.74
17	21.89	24.79
18	19.57	25.00
19	20.79	25.26
20	24.63	30.05

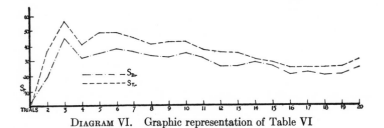

DIAGRAM VI. Graphic representation of Table VI

SECTION V

EXPERIMENTS IN MIRROR READING

The Mirror Reading Material (I.E.R.—B.L. 1 to 20) which was devised for this experiment consists of twenty pages of easy sentences given in the form of questions or directions in which every word must be read in order to answer the question or to do as directed. Each page was typed and reproduced by photo-engraving to give an offset impression which corresponded to the mirrored image of the original page. (This type of reproduction for mirror reading insures a constant stimulus page. See Figure 3.)

While the subjects read the directions silently, the experimenter read them aloud. The directions given the subject were: "This is an experiment in reading backwards given to find out how adults learn reading habits. Begin at your right and read to your left. Read each sentence carefully. Make sure that you have the thought accurately. Then write the answer in the space provided. This is usually at the left of the page. Do not think about these exercises between times. Do not practice reading this way except during the training. The scientific value of this experiment depends upon the faithful obedience to these directions. *Do not* tear this page off until the signal is given."

After reading the directions the subjects were asked, "Is that clear?" The signal "Go" was given. Sixty seconds later, the orders were given: "Stop, circle the last word. Tear off."

The page was scored for the number of letters read.

Groups practicing mirror reading on a schedule corresponding to that of the preceding experiment were equated on the basis of mean initial score.*

The A_{M_r}, A_{D_r}, and A_{T_r} symbolize the mean achievement of each group practicing under its own condition of regularly interpolating after each constant unit of practice a constant time interval of zero, of one minute, and of one day corresponding to conditions M, D, and T respectively.

---

* The characteristics of the group in relation to age, intelligence, and sampling are given in. Appendix A.

I. E. R. - B. L. -5-

1. Underline the word yes.   no yes so

2. Underscore twice the smallest number.   8 3 7 4

3. Write any number less than five.   ....

4. Underscore once the unrepeated vowel in booked.   booked

5. Underline the final letter of the word gone.   g o n e

6. Draw a square around the number that is greater than three.   2 3 6 1

7. Put a cross on the second letter of the word in the margin.   t o i n

8. Encircle the number which is the correct answer to the sum of two and five.   6 7 8 9

9. Draw a square around the number which is the quotient to the division of nine by three.   1 2 3 4

10. Write under the line the first letter of gone and the second letter of moon to form a word.   _____

11. What is the difference between the number of days in February and September in any year that is not a leap year?   ....

12. Write the word obtained by prefixing the suitable pre and suffixing the expression ted to the last two letters of the word Granada.   ....

FIGURE 3.   Specimen page of the mirror reading material
(Reduced about one-half)

The mean achievements presented in Table VII and plotted as a learning curve in Diagram VII show that under each condition of practice improvement is to be noted. Again, as in the preceding experiments, the groups practicing with the regular interpolation of an interval of time between successive practices have achieved more at each trial than the group practicing under massed conditions.

The observed superiority of each type of distribution is given by the relationship

$$S_{D_r} = A_{D_r} - A_{M_r}$$
$$S_{T_r} = A_{T_r} - A_{M_r}.$$

These observed superiorities are given in Table VIII and graphed in Diagram VIII.

TABLE VII. The mean score (and the sigma of the mean) derived from the experiment with three groups practicing mirror reading under condition of regularly interpolating after each trial a constant time interval of M, D, or T (zero, one minute, and one day, respectively).

	Mean Achievement			Standard Deviation of the Mean		
	M	D	T	M	D	T
Trial		The interval regularly interpolated after each trial				
	Zero	One Minute	One Day	Zero	One Minute	One Day
1	80.89	80.46	80.64	8.93	10.86	7.90
2	100.63	109.65	112.48	8.29	9.27	8.81
3	114.00	122.27	131.40	8.76	12.14	12.00
4	113.47	125.88	134.40	8.01	11.47	12.34
5	118.11	128.08	140.48	8.00	9.06	11.90
6	137.71	162.27	166.60	7.48	7.07	10.13
7	140.11	161.69	188.96	9.31	10.97	9.05
8	111.08	129.31	143.04	6.14	7.68	9.68
9	139.24	159.58	168.24	6.84	8.60	11.31
10	159.18	179.15	195.00	6.51	10.38	12.08
11	153.50	175.92	190.48	8.07	11.59	12.61
12	154.76	172.31	199.00	9.20	11.49	13.33
13	173.45	207.73	227.65	11.57	14.81	15.49
14	168.24	202.19	232.82	9.22	13.09	16.73
15	157.76	191.58	216.18	9.93	9.55	10.63
16	172.03	197.15	231.91	7.91	11.51	14.06
17	144.76	172.31	219.32	8.96	8.14	12.31
18	172.26	196.15	236.73	9.93	10.26	10.75
19	139.76	154.42	223.14	9.19	13.87	12.63
20	143.50	161.65	203.32	6.63	9.52	9.35

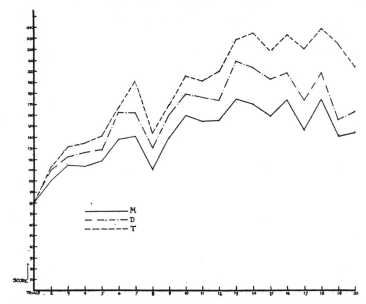

DIAGRAM VII. The mean score derived from the experiment with three groups practicing mirror reading under condition of regularly interpolating after each trial a constant time interval of *M*, *D*, or *T* (zero, one minute, and one day, respectively).

The curve of observed superiority for the *T* group over the group at each trial shows that the superiority, in general, is being augmented after each interpolated interval.

The curve of observed superiority of the *D* group shows that observed superiority, in general, is being augmented after each interpolation of time up to and including the fifteenth trial. Subsequent to the fifteenth trial, however, the observed superiority is being diminished.

Do these observations indicate that while every interpolation of an interval of twenty-four hours shows a corresponding increase in observed superiority, intervals of one minute duration may have a negative effect after the fifteenth trial?

The observations on the basis of the Snoddy data and those derived from the two experiments reported so far are not in agreement.

Since the observations derived from the experiments so far reported have not been in agreement, another function, memorizing nonsense numbers, was selected for further experimentation.

TABLE VIII. The observed superiority of achievement under condition of regularly interpolating a constant time interval of duration D and T (one minute and one day respectively) after each trial over the achievement under condition of massing. The achievements were the scores derived from the experiment in mirror reading.

Trial	S_{D_r}	S_{T_r}
1	—.43	—.25
2	9.02	11.85
3	8.27	17.40
4	12.41	20.93
5	9.97	22.37
6	24.56	28.89
7	21.58	48.85
8	18.23	32.76
9	20.45	29.00
10	19.97	35.82
11	22.42	46.98
12	17.55	35.24
13	34.28	54.20
14	33.95	64.58
15	33.82	58.42
16	25.12	59.88
17	27.55	74.56
18	23.89	64.47
19	14.66	83.38
20	18.15	60.18

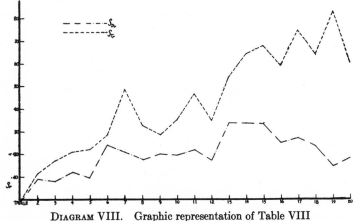

DIAGRAM VIII.   Graphic representation of Table VIII

SECTION VI

EXPERIMENTS IN MEMORIZING

The Nonsense Number Material (I.E.R.—Ass. T. 1 to 20) prepared for this experiment consists of twenty pages of numbers to be associated. The association was between a three-place number and a sequent two-place number. Twelve of these

I. E. R.—Association Test

866	79
956	31
457	78
135	23
252	68
314	51
471	29
847	33
639	24
532	76
218	45
569	12

FIGURE 4-a.   Nonsense number material to be memorized

I. E. R.—Association Test 19a

135	....
218	....
252	....
314	....
457	....
471	....
532	....
569	....
639	....
847	....
866	....
956	....

FIGURE 4-b.   Test of memorization of nonsense number material

pairs appeared on a page (see Figure 4-a).   The subjects were allowed one minute to study each page, after which they were tested by being given the three-place numbers in an order other than that of the original (see Figure 4-b).   A response of the sequent two-place number was required.   One minute was allowed for

recall.   The directions were: "This is an experiment to see how
people connect two events.   You will be given a list of numbers in
pairs which you are to learn.   Use any method you wish in studying these pairs.   You have one minute to learn each list.   You
may go over the list as often as you have time.   Afterwards
you will be given a test containing a list of the first members of
these paired series, and you are to respond by writing beside each
number the second number of the pair.   For instance,

8649   823

would be tested by giving you 8649 to which you should respond
by writing 823.

8649   . . . .

Do not tear this page off until the signal is given."

After reading the directions the experimenter asked the subject,
"Is that clear?"   After a pause to answer any question, the
order "Go" was given.   At the end of one minute, the subject
was told to stop.   The number of correct associations was the
score for the page.

Practicing the memorization of nonsense numbers were three
groups who were equated on the basis of the score of the first
page of the material.   These three groups practiced under the
conditions of regular interpolation after each constant unit of
practice, of constant time intervals of zero, one minute, and one
day.   The conditions correspond to those of the preceding experiment of *M*, *D*, and *T*.*

The achievement of each group (Table IX) shows some slight
improvement, although the distinction between *M* and *D* and *M*
and *T* is not maintained (Diagram IX).   The true extent of the
improvement may be obscured by the grossness of the measure
of achievement.

The relationships

$$S_{Dr} = A_{Dr} - A_{Mr}$$
$$S_{Tr} = A_{Tr} - A_{Mr},$$

showing the observed superiority attributable respectively to
condition *D* and *T* over *M*, were obtained trial for trial.

* The characteristics of the equated groups are given in Appendix A.

TABLE IX. The mean raw score (and the sigma of the mean raw score) derived from the experiment with three groups memorizing nonsense numbers under condition of regularly interpolating after each unit of practice constant time intervals of duration *M*, *D*, and *T* (zero, one minute, and one day, respectively).

	Mean Achievement			Standard Deviation of the Mean		
	M	*D*	*T*	*M*	*D*	*T*
	Interval regularly interpolated after each trial					
Trial	Zero	One Minute	One Day	Zero	One Minute	One Day
1	1.81	1.80	1.81	.22	.29	.31
2	1.48	2.05	2.38	.23	.27	.32
3	1.59	1.75	2.00	.21	.25	.27
4	1.89	2.10	2.73	.25	.27	.23
5	1.81	2.50	2.35	.28	.34	.21
6	1.89	2.80	2.73	.24	.27	.25
7	2.30	2.95	3.04	.23	.30	.28
8	2.52	3.15	3.15	.29	.37	.30
9	3.37	3.35	3.80	.32	.32	.32
10	2.22	3.30	2.76	.23	.33	.32
11	2.00	2.90	3.20	.28	.39	.33
12	2.33	2.60	3.24	.30	.33	.34
13	2.26	2.50	3.25	.24	.34	.31
14	2.93	3.15	3.87	.27	.39	.27
15	2.56	2.90	2.62	.29	.40	.31
16	2.44	2.30	2.87	.25	.33	.23
17	2.15	1.95	3.50	.30	.29	.32
18	2.59	2.85	3.58	.30	.34	.35
19	1.89	2.55	2.79	.28	.25	.23
20	2.93	3.05	3.96	.25	.34	.30

DIAGRAM IX. Graphic representation of Table IX

The superiorities given in Table X and represented by the curve of Diagram X show that D over M is slightly and irregularly superior and, if anything, decreases in amount of superiority on the whole. (The sums by 5-trial groups are 1.54, 3.25, 1.97, and .70.) T is superior to M throughout and on the whole increasingly so. (The sums by 5-trial groups are 2.89, 3.18, 4.10, and 4.70.)

TABLE X. The observed superiority of achievement under condition of regularly interpolating a constant time interval of duration D and T (one minute and one day respectively) after each trial over the achievement under condition of massing. The achievements were the scores derived from the experiment in associating nonsense number pairs.

Trial	S_{D_r}	S_{T_r}
1	$-.01$	.00
2	.57	.90
3	.16	.61
4	.21	.84
5	.61	.54
6	.91	.84
7	.65	.74
8	.63	.63
9	$-.02$	.43
10	1.08	.54
11	.90	1.20
12	.27	.91
13	.24	.99
14	.22	.94
15	.34	.06
16	$-.14$	.43
17	$-.20$	1.35
18	.26	.99
19	.66	.90
20	.12	1.03

DIAGRAM X. Graphic representation of Table X

SECTION VII

EXPERIMENTS IN SUBSTITUTION

Still another experiment under corresponding conditions of practice was conducted on another type of material.

I. E. R.—C. L.

For:	a	b	c	d	e	f	g	h	i	j	k	l	m
Write:	g	t	y	r	l	j	w	p	v	c	u	n	h

For:	n	o	p	q	r	s	t	u	v	w	x	y	z
Write:	a	z	s	m	f	x	q	k	d	e	o	i	b

Few orators belonging to the Church of England have acquired so great a reputation as Liddon. Others may have surpassed him in originality, learning or reasoning power, but for grasp of his subject, clearness of language, lucidity of arrangement, felicity of illustration, vividness of imagination, elegance of diction, and above all, for sympathy with the intellectual position of those whom he addressed, he has hardly been rivalled.

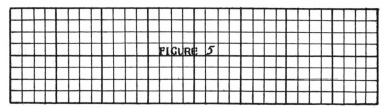

FIGURE 5

Fig. 5. A page of code substitution material

The Code Substitution Material (I.E.R.—C.L. 1 to 20) which was compiled for this experiment consists of twenty pages. At the top of each page is the Tilton Code, a letter for letter code, and a selection taken from the *Encyclopedia Britannica* to be transcribed into the code. Each page reproduced by multigraph was mounted on quadrille-ruled paper so that the subject could record each letter in a quarter-inch square (see Figure 5). Mimeographed copies of the directions were read silently by the subjects while the experimenter read them aloud. The directions were: "This is an experiment to see how people use a letter code. On the page that follows there will appear a code and some

27

TABLE XI.   The mean score (and the sigma of the mean) derived from the experiment with three groups practicing code substitution under condition of regularly interpolating after each trial, a constant time interval of *M, D,* or *T* (zero, one minute, and one day respectively).

	Mean Achievement			Standard Deviation of the Mean		
	M	*D*	*T*	*M*	*D*	*T*
		Interval regularly interpolated after each trial				
Trial	Zero	One Minute	One Day	Zero	One Minute	One Day
1	12.95	12.94	12.91	.94	1.18	1.01
2	17.13	19.39	18.35	1.03	.83	1.07
3	19.00	21.78	20.61	1.57	.86	1.08
4	20.33	23.33	21.00	1.69	.91	1.14
5	21.17	24.83	22.48	1.23	1.03	1.07
6	22.25	26.56	23.96	1.39	1.04	1.20
7	23.33	27.83	25.65	1.29	1.15	1.31
8	23.71	28.61	25.78	1.31	1.56	1.12
9	21.29	25.22	24.70	1.37	1.56	1.12
10	24.75	29.44	28.26	1.39	1.06	1.14
11	22.38	29.33	27.57	1.42	1.25	.99
12	23.38	30.50	28.04	1.47	1.54	1.25
13	22.50	28.22	26.70	1.26	.87	.88
14	25.29	31.39	30.74	1.54	1.16	1.00
15	24.96	30.11	29.96	1.46	1.05	.85
16	25.00	30.50	29.57	1.49	1.29	.98
17	25.54	30.11	29.83	1.58	1.33	1.19
18	26.71	30.77	31.04	1.97	1.68	.96
19	24.29	30.00	29.18	1.65	1.42	1.12
20	25.92	32.89	31.87	1.67	1.43	.96

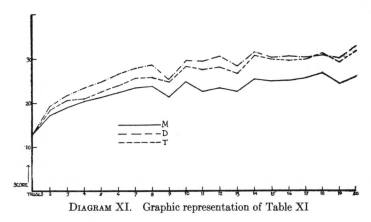

DIAGRAM XI.   Graphic representation of Table XI

material to be written in the code. Below the material to be coded is the cross-section paper on which you are to write, putting in each quarter-inch square the appropriate code letter, translating from the paragraph. Leave no blank square between words or sentences. Omit all punctuation. Work as fast as you can without making mistakes. *Do not* tear this page off until the signal is given."

After reading the directions the experimenter asked the subject, "Is that clear?" After a pause to answer any question, the order "Go" was given. The subjects were told to stop at the end of one minute.

The number of letters correctly transcribed constituted the score of the page.

The three groups, M, D, and T, which were equated* on the basis of mean score on the first page of the code substitution material, practiced under conditions of regular interpolation after each constant unit of practice of a constant time interval of zero, one minute, and one day.

The achievements A_{M_r}, A_{D_r}, and A_{T_r} are given in Table XI and graphed in Diagram XI. The learning curves show improvement under each condition of practice although the groups working under D and T achieve more at each trial than does the group working under condition M.

The observed superiority given by the relationships,

$$S_{D_r} = A_{D_r} - A_{M_r}$$
$$S_{T_r} = A_{T_r} - A_{M_r},$$

are given in Table XII and represented by the curves of Diagram XII.

The superiority of conditions D and T over M is to be noted at trial 2, and this observed superiority is, in general, augmented at every subsequent trial of the series.

It is especially interesting to note at this point that the interval of one minute is more efficient, when the results are measured in terms of number of letters coded, than is the interval of one day. A distinction must be made between the advantageous effect of time and the deleterious effect of time. One of the probable reasons for the lowered efficiency of the daily interval is the fact of the forgetting of the code.

* See Appendix A for the basis of equating groups.

TABLE XII. The observed superiority of achievement under condition of regularly interpolating a constant time interval of duration D and T (one minute and one day respectively) after each trial over the achievement under condition of massing. The achievements were the scores derived from the experiment in code substitution.

Trial	S_{D_r}	S_{T_r}
1	− .01	− .04
2	2.26	1.22
3	2.78	1.61
4	2.00	.67
5	3.66	1.31
6	4.31	1.71
7	4.50	2.32
8	4.90	2.07
9	3.93	3.41
10	3.69	3.51
11	6.95	5.19
12	7.12	4.66
13	5.72	4.20
14	5.90	5.45
15	5.15	5.00
16	5.50	4.57
17	4.57	4.29
18	4.06	4.33
19	5.71	4.89
20	6.97	5.95

DIAGRAM XII.   Graphic representation of Table XII

SECTION VIII

RÉSUMÉ AND ANALYSIS OF EXPERIMENTS

In addition to the two analyses of the Snoddy data, four experiments were conducted under conditions of regular distribution.

These conditions have been symbolized by M, D, and T, where:

Condition M represents a group practicing a function under massing.

Condition D represents a group practicing a function under regular interpolation of a constant interval of one minute after each constant unit of practice.

Condition T represents a group practicing a function under regular interpolation of a constant interval of twenty-four hours after each constant unit of practice.

The superiority of conditions T and D over condition M has been given by the relationships

$$S_{D_r} = A_{D_r} - A_{M_r}$$
$$S_{T_r} = A_{T_r} - A_{M_r}.$$

For different functions, and for different criteria within the same function, the trend of observed superiority has not been the same.

To recapitulate the observations of the preceding sections, Table XIII shows the trend of the observed superiority in the different functions.

Up to this point, continued superiority at trials subsequent to the second has been considered an indication that such superiority was dependent not only on the interval intervening between first and second trial, but also on the added effect of succeeding intervals on subsequent trials. If the superiority noted at trials subsequent to the second was less, it was assumed to indicate that the succeeding intervals had either a zero or a definitely negative effect.

For instance, the data derived from Snoddy's experiment showed superiority at trial 2, with superiority being gradually

31

TABLE XIII.   Summarizing the general findings on the basis of the four experiments conducted in this investigation, and the findings from the analysis of the raw score data of Snoddy [1926].

Function	Condition of Interpolation	Superiority at Trial 2	Superiority at Trials Subsequent to the Second
Stabilimeter (analysis of raw scores derived from Snoddy) ['26, Table 2, p. 7]	D	Marked	Diminishing from trials 2 to 20.
	T	Marked	Diminishing from trials 2 to 20.
Stabilimeter raw scores derived from reported experiment on 90° rotated maze	D	Marked	Augmented at trial 3, but diminishing from trials 4 to 20.
	T	Marked	Augmented at trial 3, but diminishing from trials 4 to 20.
Mirror Reading	D	Marked	Augmented, in general, from trials 3 to 15, diminishing from trials 16 to 20.
	T	Marked	Augmented, in general, from trials 3 to 20.
Nonsense Numbers	D	Some	Variable, in some instances inferiority.
	T	Some	Variable.
Code Substitution	D	Marked	Augmented, in general, from trials 3 to 20.
	T	Marked	Augmented, in general, from trials 3 to 20.

DIAGRAM XIII.   Representation of the theoretical trend of achievements under conditions of distribution and of massing lessened at subsequent trials. Do the observations substantiate the conclusion that the interpolated interval has an effect only after the first trial, but not after trials 2 and 3 and 4? Or does the observation on the experiment presented in Section IV on the same apparatus rotated through an angle of 90° indicate that the interpolated interval has an influence at trial 2 and at trial 3, but not at trials 4 through 20? Or does the observation on the mirror reading material indicate that the twenty-four hour interval has an effect at all trials subsequent to the first, whereas the one minute interval has no further effect after the fifteenth trial?

Benefit of distribution, in all probability, depends upon the material used in the learning experiment. In general, distribution has some advantageous aspect. The question is "Does this benefit due to the regularly interpolated interval cease at some trial during the series?"

In general, if the achievements of equal groups operating under different conditions of regular distribution of a constant time interval are graphed as learning curves, four possible sets of curves are obtained.

Let condition M be the condition of learning in which no, or a zero, interval is regularly interpolated after each constant unit of practice, and let condition J represent the condition of learning in which some constant time interval of duration J is regularly interpolated after each constant unit of practice. Furthermore, let the curve derived from the practice on any function under condition M always be the same, then A_{J_r} may have a rate of increment which

    (a) is equal to the corresponding rate of M at every trial;
    (b) is greater than the corresponding rate of M at every trial throughout the series;
    (c) is greater than the corresponding rate of M at every trial up to and including trial k, after which the rate equals that of M at every trial;
    (d) is greater than the corresponding rate of M at every trial up to and including trial k, after which the rate is sequentially less than that of M at every subsequent trial.

    (See Diagram XIII.)

The observed superiority of A_{J_r} over A_{M_r} at each trial would give, when plotted sequentially against trials, four curves of observed superiority corresponding to the four possibilities

indicated in the preceding paragraph. Each of these possibilities has as an analogue a curve which would
  (A) tend to coincide with the base line;
  (B) tend to rise continually from the base line;
  (C) tend to rise from the base line to some level of difference and maintain that level;
  (D) tend to rise from the base line during initial trials and fall toward the base line at later stages.

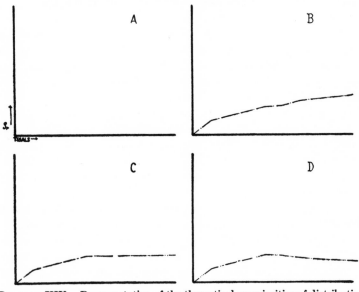

DIAGRAM XIV.   Representation of the theoretical superiorities of distribution over massing

When the curve of observed superiority for distribution shows, in general, no differences from the massing curve, there is, of course, no effect of the interval of time J observable at trial 2 or at subsequent trials.   (Aa)

When the curve of observed superiority indicates that the superiority is becoming greater and greater after each regular interpolation, there is no doubt that each interval augments the observed advantage of distribution at the preceding trial.   (Bb)

When the curve of superiority for distribution rises and then maintains its level, there is a noticeable effect of the interval up to the point where the difference in favor of D becomes uniform as in the preceding condition. But does the fact that the differences in favor of superiority are uniform indicate that the interval has a zero effect? (Cc)

If the graph of the difference in favor of the condition of distribution rises up to the kth trial and descends toward the base at trials $(k+1)$ through to n, does that fact indicate that up to the kth trial the interval had a beneficial effect, and that the effect of interval at interpolations after the kth trial is negative? (Dd)

Considering the case where observed superiority diminishes at trials subsequent to the kth, does the loss of superiority indicate the ineffectiveness of the time interval that is interpolated after trial k and after $(k+1)$ and after $(k+2)$ and so on to the interpolation after $(n-1)$th trial?

Or can a time interval, perhaps, still have a beneficial effect even when the observed superiority after an interpolation of time is lessened?

Benefit has been considered demonstrated if there is an increment in observed superiority at a subsequent trial. If observed superiority is increased at a trial succeeding an interpolation, it may be assumed that such increment is attributable to the differentiating effect of the interpolated interval. But, if observed superiority is diminished at some trial succeeding an interpolated interval, may it be assumed that the decrement is attributable to the differentiating factor of the interpolated interval? Has the time interval a negative effect?

What results would be obtained if a group practiced a function under regular distribution of an interval T to some trial r at which the superiority observed was less than that observed at trial $(r-1)$ as measured from the achievement of the group that practiced under massed conditions,—and then practiced trials r to n under massing conditions?

1. If time intervals have no effect at trials subsequent to r, the trend of the achievement ought to follow that obtained for the curve that operated under distribution J from trial r on. The curve representing the achievement of the group doing mixed practice should be identical with the curve of the achievement of the group practicing continuously under distribution of time interval J.

2. But if time intervals have a positive effect at trials subsequent to r, then the achievement of the mixed practice group

ought to be less than the achievement of the regular distribution group at trials subsequent to r.   In other words, the superiority of the mixed practice group over the massing group ought to be less at trial r through n than the superiority of the regular distribution group over the massed.

3. But if time intervals have a negative effect at trials subsequent to r, then the achievement at trials subsequent to r of the group having mixed practice ought to be greater than that of the regular distribution group.   In other words, the superiority of the mixed group over the massed group ought to be greater than the superiority of the distributed group over the massed group at trials subsequent to r.

SECTION IX

EXPERIMENT WITH MIXED PRACTICE

Using the stabilimeter presented so that four of the lanes to be traced are parallel with the horizontal axis of the subject, a group was practiced under the condition of distribution in which a constant time interval of one minute was interpolated regularly after each unit of practice from trial 1 to trial 5. From the sixth

TABLE XIV. The mean score (and the sigma of the mean) derived from an experiment with a group practicing the rotated stabilimeter under condition of regularly interpolating a one minute interval after trials 1, 2, 3, 4, and 5, and then continuing the practice on trials 6 to 20 under massing. In addition the means derived from the experiment on the same apparatus (reported in Section IV) under conditions of regularly interpolating a constant time interval of zero and one minute after each unit of practice are given below for comparison.

Mean Achievement of Group

Trial	X One minute interval after trials 1, 2, 3, 4, 5, trials 6 to 20 massed	D One Minute	M Zero	Standard Devia- tion from Mean of X Group
1	161.6	161.4	162.7	13.5
2	123.4	131.3	150.4	12.2
3	103.1	98.9	144.1	9.5
4	87.4	88.8	120.6	10.0
5	74.8	76.1	111.6	4.7
6	68.6	71.5	110.1	5.6
7	73.1	69.0	105.0	8.8
8	71.3	63.7	97.2	6.9
9	72.3	62.5	94.8	8.0
10	73.4	58.0	93.0	9.8
11	72.6	56.2	87.8	6.9
12	71.1	56.7	82.7	6.0
13	68.8	57.6	83.7	4.0
14	72.1	49.8	78.8	6.1
15	62.2	50.8	75.9	3.6
16	61.7	51.5	72.3	4.5
17	67.0	48.7	70.6	6.9
18	68.4	49.8	69.2	7.2
19	64.5	46.9	67.7	4.1
20	65.6	47.3	71.9	4.6

trial until the twentieth the condition of practice was changed to that of massing so that no interval was interpolated between any trials subsequent to the sixth trial.

The achievements of this group (Table XIV) were plotted against trials, and for comparison the corresponding curves derived under condition *M* and condition *D* in the experiment reported in Section IV are also plotted in Diagram XV. Let the symbol *X* represent the condition of massed practice so that

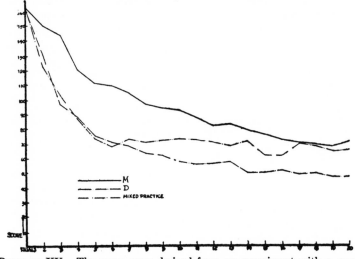

DIAGRAM XV. The mean score derived from an experiment with a group practicing the rotated stabilimeter under condition of regularly interpolating a one minute interval after trials 1, 2, 3, 4, and 5, and then continuing the practice on trials 6 to 20 under massing. In addition the means derived from the experiment on the same apparatus (reported in Section IV) under condition of regularly interpolating a constant time interval of zero and one minute after each unit of practice are given above for comparison.

A_X, represents the achievement at trial *r* of the group having mixed practice.

There will be noted a high consistency between A_D and A_X at trials 1, 2, 3, 4, 5, and 6. After trial 6, however, the change in trend is abrupt and consistent for the *X* group.

The *X* group does improve with trials subsequent to the sixth, but compared to the improvement of the *D* group at the corresponding trials, the loss in superiority at trials 7 through 20 is consistent.

As a result of this experiment, benefit due to the interpolation of intervals of time at trials subsequent to the sixth has been demonstrated.   The interpolated time interval has an effect, and that effect seems consistent.   The difference between A_D and A_X at trials subsequent to the sixth may give some indication of the value of successive interpolations of interval.

TABLE XV.   The superiority of the achievement of the group having intervals of one minute regularly interpolated after each trial over the achievement of the group having the same condition of practice up to the trial after which the condition was changed to massing.   Comparison given from trial 6 at which conditions were changed.

Trial	S_r
6	−2.9
7	4.1
8	7.6
9	9.8
10	15.4
11	16.4
12	14.4
13	11.2
14	12.3
15	11.4
16	10.2
17	18.3
18	18.6
19	17.6
20	18.3

This experiment shows that the criterion of observed superiority is not a necessary condition to demonstrate benefit attributable to regular interpolation of time interval.*

* The rate of improvement following a change in conditions of practice is not attributable to any disturbance sequent to such change. See Appendix C.

SECTION X

COMPARISON OF ONE MINUTE AND
ONE DAY INTERVALS

Up to this point, the only base of reference for ascertaining superiority has been the M curve. If, however, two types of distribution are compared, the observed superiority of one over the other may be measured.

TABLE XVI. The superiority of achievement under condition of interpolating a regular interval of twenty-four hours after each trial over the achievement under condition when such interval is one minute. The achievements are the raw scores derived from the experiment on the rotated stabilimeter.

Trial	W_{T_r}
1	-1.47
2	17.37
3	11.74
4	9.05
5	12.95
6	10.32
7	9.37
8	7.47
9	10.21
10	7.37
11	5.56
12	9.68
13	8.79
14	1.89
15	3.53
16	6.95
17	2.89
18	5.63
19	4.47
20	5.42

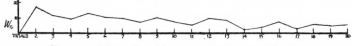

DIAGRAM XVI. Graphic representation of Table XVI

40

In the practice on the stabilimeter, in learning backward reading, and, to a certain degree, in the memorization of nonsense numbers, condition T has been superior to condition D, i.e., achievement when the duration of the constant time interval was twenty-four hours at each regular interpolation has been greater than achievement when the duration of the constant time interval was one minute. Let the symbol W_{T_r} represent the relationship

$$W_{T_r} = A_{T_r} - A_{D_r}$$

so that, in effect, W is a measure of the superiority of one condition of regular distribution over another. The plot of each of these superiorities W for each type of material then will give the trend of the superiority of one constant interval over another.

Table XVI gives the W obtained for the rotated stabilimeter experiment. The plot of W_D for these data is represented in Diagram XVI.

It will be noted that the observed superiority at trial 2 is at maximum. Can the later diminished superiorities indicate that the addition of 1,439 minutes to a one-minute interval has a negative effect? On the contrary, when the superiority W_{T_r} for the difference in achievement on the mirror reading material (Table XVII) is graphed, there is seen a constantly augmented curve indicating superiority as becoming greater and greater after each interpolation (Diagram XVII).

When the superiority W_{T_r} (Table XVIII) is graphed for the nonsense numbers, the trend (Diagram XVIII) of observed superiority is first for greater superiority, then diminishes to inferiority, but after the eleventh trial the trend is toward greater observed superiority.

In the code learning material, the superior interval is of duration D, or one minute. Plotting the trend of the superiority (Table XIX),

$$W_{D_r} = A_{D_r} - A_{T_r},$$

the superiority rises in general to trial 12. After trial 12, however, the trend is toward diminishing superiority (Diagram XIX).

It is probable that the effect of time operates (1) to make the process of learning more satisfying or more easily attended to and (2) to make for forgetting.

With the code learning material, the observed superiority of

TABLE XVII. The superiority of achievement of interpolating a regular interval of twenty-four hours after each trial over the achievement under condition when such interval is one minute. The achievements were derived from the experiment with the mirror reading materials.

Trial	W_{T_r}
1	.18
2	2.83
3	9.13
4	8.52
5	12.40
6	4.33
7	27.27
8	14.53
9	8.66
10	15.85
11	14.56
12	26.69
13	19.92
14	30.63
15	24.60
16	34.76
17	47.01
18	40.58
19	68.72
20	41.67

DIAGRAM XVII.   Graphic representation of Table XVII

the D and T groups over the M group was indicated by the relationship

$$S_{D_r} = A_{D_r} - A_{M_r}$$
$$S_{T_r} = A_{D_r} - A_{M_r}.$$

The trend of both observed superiorities has been shown (Diagram XI, Section VII) to be towards increasing the superiority at each trial, whereas the relationship

$$W_{D_r} = A_{D_r} - A_{T_r},$$

which shows the superiority of the regular interpolation of a constant interval of one minute over that of twenty-four hours, does not show a generally increasing superiority at each subsequent trial. On the contrary, after the twelfth trial the superiorities tend to become less and less, so that in at least one instance the superiority is for twenty-four hours.

The curve of A_{D_r} and A_{T_r} for the code substitution shows that the achievements are becoming more and more nearly alike at trials subsequent to the thirteenth trial.

TABLE XVIII. The superiority of achievement under condition of interpolating a regular interval of twenty-four hours after each trial over the achievement under condition when such interpolation is one minute. The achievements are the scores derived from the experiment in memorizing nonsense numbers.

Trial	W_{T_r}
1	.01
2	.33
3	.25
4	.63
5	—.15
6	—.07
7	.09
8	.00
9	.45
10	—.54
11	.30
12	.64
13	.75
14	.72
15	.72
16	.57
17	1.55
18	.73
19	.24
20	.91

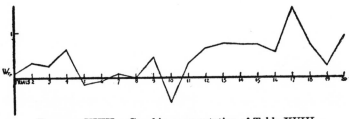

DIAGRAM XVIII. Graphic representation of Table XVIII

It has been demonstrated that the interval may still have a beneficial effect despite the fact that the superiority is diminishing after the kth trial.   Then why should there be diminished superiority?

If regular distribution is beneficial at all, the group practicing under the condition of distribution will reach either a plateau or a limit of practical achievement in fewer units of practice than the group working under the condition of massing.   When such a plateau or limit of practical achievement has been reached, then after each additional interpolation of time the amount of improvement possible under the condition of distribution is less than that of the massed practice group; the possibilities of further improvement are greater for the massed practice group.   Hence,

TABLE XIX.   The superiority of achievement under condition of interpolating a regular interval of one minute after each trial over the achievement under condition when such interpolation is twenty-four hours.   The achievements are derived from the experiment in code substitution.

Trial	W_{D_r}
1	.03
2	1.04
3	1.17
4	2.33
5	2.35
6	2.60
7	2.18
8	2.83
9	.52
10	1.18
11	1.76
12	2.46
13	1.52
14	.65
15	.15
16	.93
17	.28
18	—.27
19	.82
20	1.02

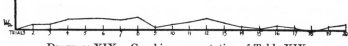

DIAGRAM XIX.   Graphic representation of Table XIX

after the limit of practical achievement has been reached, the group working under distribution will improve at a rate that is tending toward a zero rate of improvement, while the rate of improvement of the massing group will be greater, trial for trial, than the corresponding rate of the distributed practice group. Hence, observed superiority in favor of a distributed practice group will become less until eventually such superiority becomes zero.

After the twelfth trial, the achievements of the D and T groups are tending to the same limit. This fact may illustrate that after practical limit is reached the observed superiority diminishes.

In the stabilimeter data, evidence of the achievement curves shows that again the two curves derived under D and T are tending to approach one another rapidly. The major part of the improvement is made early in the series, and with reference to the possibility of further improvement the distribution curves decelerate more rapidly than the M curve with its greater possibilities of improvement.

It can be said that the superiority possible under the successive interpolations of a constant time interval has been obscured by the limits of practical achievement of the material.

When the material is such that the limit of achievement is not only not reached but not approached, then, of course, the differences will be constantly increasing, demonstrating the augmented superiority due to each interpolated interval. Such seems to be the case with the mirror reading material where the D and T distribution curves show constantly increasing differences.

SECTION XI

THE EFFECT OF THE INTERPOLATION OF A SINGLE INTERVAL

It has been shown that augmented observed superiority is not a necessary condition to demonstrate a beneficial aspect of time interval. Is it a sufficient condition?

Since the additional interpolation of interval is the only factor of difference between the massed group and the distributed group, to interpolation must be attributed the effect of the augmented superiority, unless augmented superiority makes for augmented superiority in and of itself.

If the condition of practice is changed from distribution to massing, after distribution has been allowed to differentiate the group operating under mixed practice from that working under massing, it is possible that the group operating under mixed practice

1. will continue to improve in achievement at the same rate as the regular distribution group.
2. will continue to improve in achievement at a rate greater than that of the regular distribution group.
3. will not continue to improve at a rate the same as, or greater than, that of the regular distribution group, but at a rate approaching that of the continuous practice group.

If possibility 1 obtains, additional interpolations of time are of zero value.

If possibility 2 obtains, additional interpolations of interval are of negative value.

If possibility 3 obtains, additional interpolations are of positive value.

Possibilities 1 and 2 may be interpreted as meaning that maintenance of the rate of the regular distribution group or improvement at a rate in excess of that of the regular distribution group is dependent upon the rate of improvement that obtained

46

at the trial at which the massing condition was substituted for distribution.

Table XX.   The mean score (and the sigma of the mean) of the group practicing code substitution under condition of having one interpolation of a one minute interval after the first trial, after which interpolation trials 2 to 20 are taken under massed practice.   The achievements of the group practicing continually under massing are presented for comparison (Section VII, Table XI).

Trial	X Interval of one minute after trial 1; then trials 2 to 20 continue massed	M	Standard Deviation of Mean of X
1	12.91	12.95	1.42
2	18.78	17.13	1.13
3	20.91	19.00	1.09
4	20.39	20.33	.89
5	21.87	21.17	.93
6	22.96	22.25	1.01
7	23.48	23.33	.80
8	23.78	23.71	.97
9	21.91	21.29	.90
10	24.74	24.75	1.10
11	24.50	22.38	.94
12	24.32	23.38	1.05
13	23.36	22.50	.82
14	25.82	25.29	.98
15	25.56	24.96	.96
16	25.32	25.00	.85
17	24.82	25.54	.96
18	25.82	26.71	1.05
19	24.36	24.29	.98
20	24.73	25.92	1.25

Diagram XX.   Graphic representation of Table XX

An experiment attacking that problem was conducted on the code substitution material under the following condition: an interval of one minute was interpolated between trials 1 and 2 so that the achievement at trial 2 of the group would be greater than the corresponding achievement of the M group. Thereafter trials 2 to 20 were given under massed practice.

The achievements of this group have been plotted with the achievements of the groups that practiced the code substitution without the benefit of even one interpolation of interval (Table XX).

The curves become practically identical from trial 12 on through 20.* (Diagram XX).

It cannot then be said that the reason for the superiority of a group working under distribution is greater because the group has a greater achievement at the second trial.

Augmented superiority at subsequent trials is a sufficient condition to demonstrate the effectiveness of an interpolated time interval over massed practice.

---

* The cumulated achievements from trials 12 to 20 are 224.11 and 223.59. .

SECTION XII

SUMMARY

In the experiments conducted to determine whether the efficiency attributable to the regularly interpolated time interval ceases, begins, or continues at some subsequent period of practice, the following variables were controlled:

a. Duration of the practice period.
b. Number of practice periods.
c. Duration of the interpolated time intervals.
d. Number of interpolated intervals.
e. Stage at which interpolation is introduced.

The experiments, conducted on each type of material, with the conditions of distribution, are given in Table XXI.

TABLE XXI. The conditions under which the various experiments were conducted

Material	Duration of Unit of Practice	Number of Practice Units	Duration of Interpolated Interval	Condition of Interpolation
Stabilimeter "rotated at 90°"	One trial	20	Zero	Regularly after each unit of practice.
"	"	20	One minute	Regularly after each unit of practice.
"	"	20	One day	Regularly after each unit of practice.
"	"	20	One minute and zero	One minute interval regularly after each unit of practice up to and including the fifth, then trials 6 to 20 massed.
"	"	11 *	48 hours and zero	An interval of 48 hours between trials 1 and 2, and then trials 2 to 11 massed.
"	"	10 †	One hour	Regularly after each unit of practice.

* This experiment is reported in Appendix C.
† The data for this experiment are reported in Appendix B.

Table XXI (*Continued*)

Mirror Reading	One minute	20	Zero	Regularly after each unit of practice.
	"	20	One minute	Regularly after each unit of practice.
	"	20	One day	Regularly after each unit of practice.
	"	10 *	One hour	Regularly after each unit of practice.
Nonsense Numbers	One minute	20	Zero	Regularly after each unit of practice.
	"	20	One minute	Regularly after each unit of practice.
	"	20	One day	Regularly after each unit of practice.
	"	10 *	One hour	Regularly after each unit of practice.
Code Learning	"	20	Zero	Regularly after each unit of practice.
	"	20	One minute	Regularly after each unit of practice.
	"	20	One day	Regularly after each unit of practice.
	"	20	One minute and zero	One minute interval between trials 1 and 2, trials 2 to 20 massed.
	"	10 *	One hour	Regularly after each unit of practice.

* The data for this experiment are reported in Appendix B.

All data derived from these experiments were treated by the technic of obtaining the differences between the achievements under condition of massing and the achievements at the same trial of another group under condition of distribution. This technic of differences gave a measure which was termed "observed superiority" or S_r. In a similar manner the measure of observed superiority of one type of distribution over another was given by W_r.

The trends of the S_r (or the observed superiority of achievement under regular distribution of a constant time interval over the achievement under massing) were of two types:

1. Rise in observed superiority augmented after each interpolation.

2. Rise in observed superiority augmented after each interpolation up to the kth trial (after which the observed superiority diminishes).

It has been shown that the rise in observed superiority augmented after each interpolation was a sufficient condition to demonstrate that each interpolation had an effect on subsequent achievement, although it was not a necessary condition, since it was shown that, even when the trend of the observed superiority was diminishing at subsequent trials, time interval still had a beneficial effect.

In these experiments, the general findings of distribution were substantiated, i.e., learning under the condition of distribution is more efficient than under the condition of massing. But, in addition, it was found that at each subsequent practice, the difference in achievement was attributable to the interpolated time interval since it has been shown that:

1. The differences in achievement due to a regularly interpolated time interval are not attributable to the advantage that the group under distribution have at trial 2.
2. Even in material where differences in achievement became less and less after some particular trial, the time interval still has a beneficial effect.

Since it has been demonstrated that augmented observed superiority at each subsequent trial is, in and of itself, a sufficient condition to demonstrate the effectiveness of each interpolation of interval, and since it has been demonstrated that diminished observed superiority at each subsequent trial is, in and of itself, not a sufficient condition to demonstrate the effectiveness of each interpolation of interval, it is believed that the time interval will promote an efficiency beyond that attained under massing, at least until the skill is acquired, or the fact learned, to some criterion of mastery. In other words, the limit of possible contribution of time interval is at the trial at which mastery is achieved, or at which practically complete learning is attained.

It is not contended that time interval is continuously operative. The limit of possible contribution of time interval is at the trial at which absolute mastery is achieved, or at which limit of learning is attained.

These experiments offer some evidence concerning the two most likely reasons why distribution is beneficial. They are that (1) the neural changes may in some unknown way "set" or establish themselves more fully when time is allowed them; and (2) the process of learning may be more satisfying and receive better attention when rest periods intervene. In general, we should expect little loss in satisfyingness and interest within twenty minutes of learning of any of the functions used in these experiments, except the mirror drawing, and should expect that a rest of a minute would restore the status in these respects nearly or quite as well as the rest of a day. The superiority of a minute over zero and the superiority of a day over a minute * thus support the view that the effect of the rests in distributed learning is by virtue of some process of "setting" or self-establishment.

* In the case of code substitution the effect of the long interval as an opportunity for "forgetting" apparently subtracts much from its effect as an opportunity for "setting."

APPENDIX A

DATA CONCERNING THE EQUATING OF THE GROUPS

In each of the experiments conducted on the stabilimeter, the mirror reading material, the nonsense numbers series, and the code substitution, the groups practicing under each condition were composed of students in the psychology classes in attendance at the regular winter and spring sessions in Teachers College, Columbia University, during the years 1928, 1929, and 1930.

Each subject in so far as was possible was given the I.E.R. battery Intelligence Scale CAVD in order to get an exact intelligence level score. In some instances, where administration of the CAVD was impracticable, a prediction of the CAVD score was made from the T scores derived from the General Examination, a six-hour intelligence examination required of all candidates for degrees at Teachers College.*

Age was determined from the registrar's record of year of birth.

In order to determine whether the group ought be equated on the basis of the CAVD level score, age, and initial trial, the correlations among these variables were determined for each type of material. The correlations were in every instance low, so that each group was equated on the basis of mean initial score on each material.

The correlation for each type of material is given in the table below.

	CAVD and Initial Score	Age and Initial Score	CAVD and Age
Stabilimeter	+.27	+.20	+.10
Mirror Reading	+.28	—.06	+.10
Nonsense Numbers........	+.28	+.10	+.10
Code Substitution	+.20	—.18	+.10

The mean age and CAVD level score for each group on each material were obtained. In conducting the first four experiments, four groups were used instead of the three reported in this study. These groups practiced under conditions of regular interpolation, after each constant unit of practice of time intervals of zero, one minute, one hour, and one day—conditions M, D, H, and T respectively. Appendix B presents the reasons for not considering the H group in the main discussion of results. Instead of being given twenty units of practice as had been done for M, D, and T, group H in every material was given but ten trials.

---

* This determination was made on the basis of "the line of relation" [Otis '22] for approximately twenty-five subjects. The obtained correlation between general examination and CAVD level score was .76.

The table below gives for each material the schedule and the mean CAVD and age.

Material	Time Interval Between Trials		Number of Trials	Number of Subjects	Mean CAVD	Mean Age
Stabilimeter	Zero	M	20	19	423.5	27.4
	1 minute	D	20	19	421.8	30.2
	1 hour	H	10	21	424.9	35.8
	1 day	T	20	19	419.7	31.8
Mirror Reading	Zero	M	20	37	419.4	30.3
	1 minute	D	20	27	425.0	29.1
	1 hour	H	10	18	422.1	32.0
	1 day	T	20	25	425.5	35.9
Nonsense Numbers ..	Zero	M	20	31	416.1	24.9
	1 minute	D	20	20	422.3	30.7
	1 hour	H	10	21	427.1	33.5
	1 day	T	20	26	420.9	36.3
Code Substitution ...	Zero	M	20	24	422.6	29.0
	1 minute	D	20	21	424.0	29.3
	1 hour	H	10	17	422.2	31.2
	1 day	T	20	23	421.4	34.0

APPENDIX B

EXPERIMENT WITH INTERVAL OF ONE HOUR

The group that operated under condition *H* on each material was given ten trials beginning at 9 A.M.; the last unit of practice came at 6 P.M.

					Mean Score					
Trials........	1	2	3	4	5	6	7	8	9	10
Time of Trial	9 A.M.	10 A.M.	11 A.M.	12 M.	1 P.M.	2 P.M.	3 P.M.	4 P.M.	5 P.M.	6 P.M.
Material										
Stabilimeter..	162.52	111.57	90.38	86.38	79.00	69.95	64.81	66.90	65.00	63.24
Mirror Reading........	80.33	117.56	144.11	131.33	137.00	171.78	178.94	134.00	168.11	180.33
Nonsense Numbers...	1.81	2.10	2.05	2.76	1.90	2.29	2.48	3.14	3.38	2.24
Code Substitution.....	12.94	18.59	21.29	20.59	22.29	24.00	24.65	25.71	24.71	28.06
					σ of Mean					
Stabilimeter..	17.91	6.81	4.52	6.94	4.73	4.23	3.92	3.74	4.25	5.56
Mirror Reading........	12.67	12.52	13.65	12.53	12.80	8.58	10.69	10.91	10.21	12.87
Nonsense Numbers...	.26	.23	.28	.23	.26	.28	.22	.32	.32	.19
Code Substitution.....	1.06	.91	1.20	.88	.96	.98	1.06	1.03	1.20	.89

Since only ten units of practice were given, and since a fluctuation in trend was noticed between the hours 11 and 2, the data of the *H* group are not presented in the tables.

The group practicing the stabilimeter under conditions of interpolating one minute after each trial through the fifth trial and giving subsequent practice under massing was equated to the mean of the other groups practicing the device under regular distribution. There were fourteen subjects in the group.

There were twenty-three subjects in the group practicing code learning under the condition of interpolating but one one-minute interval after trial 1.

APPENDIX C

AN EXPERIMENT WITH A SINGLE INTERVAL OF TWO DAYS

A group of eight subjects practiced the rotated stabilimeter under the following conditions: an interval of 48 hours was interpolated after trial 1; then trials 2 to 11 were given under conditions of massing. The table below represents the data under this condition of mixed practice as well as the data derived under conditions of absolute massing.

Trial	Mixed Group	Massed Practice Group	The Scores of the Massed Practice Group from Trial 8 through 17 for Comparison	
1	166.5	162.7		
2	94.9	150.4	Trial 8	94.8
3	94.8	144.1	9	93.0
4	87.9	120.6	10	87.8
5	94.9	111.6	11	82.7
6	85.6	110.1	12	83.7
7	81.5	105.0	13	78.8
8	80.9	94.8	14	75.9
9	73.5	93.0	15	72.2
10	73.9	87.8	16	70.5
11	75.6	82.7	17	69.1

An interval of 48 hours after trial 1 is probably more beneficial in the type of function represented by the stabilimeter than is an interval of 24 hours. The achievement after such an interpolation is approximately equivalent to that resulting after eight massed practices.

The comparison of the achievements at trials 2 to 11 of the mixed practice group with those of the absolute massing group at trials 8 to 17 is valid since both groups for that period of ten trials are operating under conditions of massing and are comparable in that the control of the maze of each group is approximately equal.

This comparison shows that, in general, the trend is the same for the two groups.

Since the trends are similar, the probabilities are that the abrupt break in the curve is not attributable to any disturbing factor sequent to a change in conditions of practice.

The data seem to indicate that the rates of improvement for a group having equal control of the maze, operating under the same conditions of practice, are approximately equal.

APPENDIX D

REFERENCES

'22 OTIS, ARTHUR S. The Method of Finding the Correspondence between Scores on Two Tests. *Journal of Educational Psychology,* 13, 9, 529–545.

'22 WARDEN, CARL JOHN. The Distribution of Practice in Animal Learning. *Comparative Psychology Monographs,* 1, 3.

'26 SNODDY, GEORGE S. Learning and Stability. *Journal of Applied Psychology,* 10, 1, 1–36.

'28 RUCH, THEODORE C. Factors Influencing the Relative Economy of Massed and Distributed Practice in Learning. *Psychological Review,* 35, 1, 19–45.